WHAT ARE WANTS AND NEEDS?

BARBARA GOTTFRIED HOLLANDER

Britannica®
Educational Publishing

IN ASSOCIATION WITH

ROSEN
EDUCATIONAL SERVICES

To Ruthie with much love and appreciation for being you, simply amazing you.

Published in 2017 by Britannica Educational Publishing (a trademark of Encyclopædia Britannica, Inc.) in association with The Rosen Publishing Group, Inc.
29 East 21st Street, New York, NY 10010

Distributed exclusively by Rosen Publishing.
To see additional Britannica Educational Publishing titles, go to rosenpublishing.com.

First Edition

Britannica Educational Publishing
J.E. Luebering: Executive Director, Core Editorial
Mary Rose McCudden: Editor, Britannica Student Encyclopedia

Rosen Publishing
Heather Moore Niver: Editor
Nelson Sá: Art Director
Brian Garvey: Designer
Cindy Reiman: Photography Manager
Heather Moore Niver: Photo Researcher

Library of Congress Cataloging-in-Publication Data

Names: Hollander, Barbara Gottfried, 1970– author.
Title: What are wants and needs? / Barbara Gottfried Hollander.
Description: New York : Britannica Educational Pub., 2017. | Series: Let's
  find out: community economics | Audience: Grades 1–4. | Includes
  bibliographical references and index.
Identifiers: ISBN 9781680484076 (library bound)
  | ISBN 9781680484151 (pbk.) | ISBN 9781680483833 (6-pack)
Subjects: LCSH: Basic needs—Juvenile literature. | Choice
  (Psychology)—Juvenile literature.
Classification: LCC HC79.B38 H65 2016 | DDC 306—dc23
LC record available at http://lccn.loc.gov/2015051443

Manufactured in the United States of America

Cover, interior pages background image Twin Design/Shutterstock.com; p. 4 Arina P Habich/Shutterstock.com; p. 5 Syda Productions/Shutterstock.com; p. 6 issarapong srirungpanich/Shutterstock.com; p. 7 bowdenimages/iStock/Thinkstock; p. 8 luna4/iStock/Thinkstock; p. 9 monkeybusinessimages/iStock/Thinkstock; p. 10 Fuse/Thinkstock; p. 11 wavebreakmedia/Shutterstock.com; p. 12 PhotoQuest/Archive Photos/Getty Images; p. 13 Yoshikazu Tsuno/AFP/Getty Images; p. 14 Jupiterimages/Stockbyte/Thinkstock; p. 15 Wavebreakmedia Ltd/Wavebreak Media/Thinkstock; pp. 16, 22 Jupiterimages/Creatas/Thinkstock; p. 17 fotoslavt/iStock/Thinkstock; p. 18 LifesizeImages/DigitalVision/Thinkstock; p. 19 © iStockphoto.com/Aldo Murillo; p. 20 Spencer Platt/Getty Images; p. 21 Spike Mafford/Photodisc/Thinkstock; p. 23 Christian Science Monitor/Getty Images; p. 24 Ingram Publishing/Thinkstock; p. 25 MIXA next/Thinkstock; p. 26 TatyanaGI/iStock/Thinkstock; p. 27 © iStockphoto.com/letterberry; p. 28 Rawpixel.com/Shutterstock.com; p. 29 Jochen Sand/DigitalVision/Thinkstock.

CONTENTS

Do You Need It?

A healthy body needs food. Grocery stores have lots of food. You can find fruits and vegetables, like apples, oranges, bananas, and potatoes. You can also find lots of candy.

Which foods are needs? Which ones are wants? A need is something you must have to live, like water and fruits, vegetables, and other nourishing foods. A want is something you would like to have but do not need, such as candy.

Your body needs healthy foods, like fresh fruits and vegetables.

FRESH LOCAL PRODUCE

THINK ABOUT IT

The words people use affect what they think and do. How many times do you mean "want" but say the word "need"?

While some people want to eat things like cookies and potato chips, they can live without them. But the human body cannot live for more than three or four days without water.

People often want to eat doughnuts or other sweets that can harm their health.

I REALLY WANT IT!

Everyone in the world has the same basic needs. All people need nourishing food, water, shelter, and clothes. These are physical needs, or things the body must have to live.

Everyone does not have the same wants. A small child may want a toy for a birthday gift, while a teenager may prefer a dinner with friends.

Businesses make products and offer services based on both wants

Clothing is a need. Your style of clothing is a want.

Why might someone prefer a scooter to a bike—or a bike to a scooter?

and needs. They produce things that they think people need and want. Businesses also have wants and needs of their own. They want people to prefer their goods and services. They use advertising, like commercials, to persuade people to buy their products.

THINK ABOUT IT

Advertisements appear on websites, television, mobile apps, billboards, and magazines. Where do you think people your age see the most ads?

Hot or Cold?

Everyone has the same general needs, but there are still differences in those needs. For example, needs may depend on the weather where a person lives. What if you lived in a place with cold weather most of the time? What if it was warm all the time? In cold places, coats, boots, and heated houses are

People who live in areas with cold weather need clothing that keeps them warm.

"Influence" means "to affect." The weather and the place you live influence your needs and wants.

needs. In warm places, people need light clothing and shelters to protect them from the sun.

The place you live may **influence** your needs in other ways, too. If you live on a farm, you can grow your own food. If you live in a large city, you have to buy the food you need in a store.

Your needs are met in different ways. For example, you can buy your food or grow it.

How Old Are You?

Some needs depend on age or ability. A baby cannot walk into the kitchen and get food. The baby needs someone to feed her. A healthy baby grows into a teenager, who can get her own food. She still needs to eat, but she does not need someone to feed her.

Ability is how one does things. Some people are disabled. They may have trouble moving, seeing, or hearing. For example, a person may not be able to use his legs

When you were a baby, many of your physical needs were met with the help of others.

THINK ABOUT IT

How do ramps and elevators in schools help people in wheelchairs?

to walk. He may need a wheelchair to get around, and he may need help in pushing his chair.

Age and ability affect how one gets the things he or she needs. A person in a wheelchair may need more physical help than someone else.

A person in a wheelchair may need ramps to enter and exit a building.

Blast into the Past

Hundreds of years ago, people traveled by foot, ship, and horse. They did not need gas for cars, trains, and airplanes. They also did not want phones, computers, and televisions because those things did not exist!

Long ago, most people also lived on farms. They grew their own food and made the products they needed. Today, wealthy countries have businesses that provide the goods and services that most people use. They often

Hundreds of years ago, people did not want computers because they did not exist!

COMPARE AND CONTRAST

People's needs and wants change as the world changes. Compare and contrast your needs to your parents' or grandparents' when they were children.

use technology to meet needs and wants. Technology is using science to make things, like airplanes and cell phones. Technology can create more needs and wants. People used the first cell phones only to make calls. Today, many people use their phones to make calls, do work, take pictures and videos, and play games.

Technology can also help meet needs. For example, it can be used to invent ways to clean water.

Future needs, like creating clean drinking water, may be met with technology.

MONEY, MONEY, MONEY

People use money to pay for most of the things they need and want, like food, clothes, toys, going to the doctor, and getting a haircut. Each of those things costs a different amount. A piece of fruit may cost less than a dollar, but a new house is very expensive.

Most people must think about how much money they have and how they want to

People pay for goods and services, like a haircut, with money.

spend it. If they do not have enough money for their needs, they cannot pay for the things they want.

A budget can help people pay for needs first and then use some of their leftover money to pay for wants.

A **budget** is a plan for using money. It lists how much money a person has and all the wants and needs that will cost money.

People make budgets to keep track of income and expenses.

Filling needs and wants is also about knowing the difference between them. Someone may need a pair of shoes, but he does not need the most expensive pair of shoes or ten pairs. Shoes that cost a lot of money or having many pairs of shoes are wants.

You need shoes. But do you need the latest, most expensive pair?

COMPARE AND CONTRAST

Think about some of the things you want and some that you need. Which cost more?

When people confuse wants and needs, they can spend too much of their money. Then they will not have enough for their real needs.

Use your money to pay for your needs first. Use what is left over for your wants.

Do You Need It Now?

Wants and even some needs do not have to be met right away. For example, if your sister needs a new coat for next winter but does not have the money to

Figure out which needs are affordable now and which can be met in the future.

THINK ABOUT IT

How does having a budget help someone to think about saving and paying for things later?

buy one, she will have to wait to get the coat. A budget can help her think about how to pay for that in the future. Your sister may have money left over after she pays for all the things she needs right away. That may not be enough for the coat, but she can put that extra money aside. This is called saving. If she saves a little bit each month, in several months she might have enough to buy that coat.

Saving money allows you to afford things you need and want in the future.

Helping Out

Not everyone in the world can afford all the things they need. Millions of people live in places that are very poor. There are few jobs so the people cannot make money. In some places, people have less than $2.00 to live on each day. Some countries have government programs that help people pay for their needs. Universal health

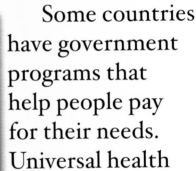

Many organizations help people in need by giving food, water, and medical care.

THINK ABOUT IT

Around 100 million people worldwide do not have a place to live. How would you feel if you did not have a home?

care plans pay for doctor's visits. Other programs help people to pay for food.

Many organizations help by giving food, water, and medical care. They may give more help when disasters, like earthquakes, happen. Individuals often help as well. They send some of their own money to

Some countries have programs that help people buy food.

21

the organizations that help. They may also volunteer their time to help collect food or clothing to send to the people who need those things.

Some places do not have access to electricity or clean water to drink, bathe, cook, and wash in. In some parts

You can volunteer to help others, like taking part in a food drive.

THINK ABOUT IT

How are your needs and wants different from those of people in other places?

of the world, girls walk long distances every day to collect water for their family. They do not have time to go to school, play, or take care of their own needs. After all their work, the water may still be dirty and make people sick.

There are places in the world where people struggle to get the freshwater they need every day.

FEELING GOOD

Food and shelter are physical needs, but people have emotional needs as well. These are things that help them to feel healthy and good inside. What makes you feel good?

Feeling loved, safe, supported, and cared for can make you feel good. Believing in yourself, knowing how to solve problems, and getting respect also

Friends can help fill your emotional needs by making you feel happy and supported.

make you feel good. Respect is being treated well.

You can fill your own emotional needs by loving, respecting, and supporting yourself. Other people can also fill these needs, like a parent who loves you or a friend who shows you respect.

Family members can provide emotional support by showing love and respect.

The choices you make decide if you fill your emotional needs. For example, you can choose friends who treat people nicely. You can also choose to cross the street safely. These choices make you feel cared for, respected, and safe.

Emotional needs are those that have to do with feelings.

Think about a time when you were hungry. How did you feel? Hunger affects how people think, grow, and act with other people. Being hungry for a long time can make people sick.

Feeling sad, unsafe, or unloved also has bad effects on how someone thinks, grows, and acts. Filling physical needs is about staying alive. Emotional needs are about how someone lives.

By taking care of

How does being sad make you feel inside? How does it affect your actions?

physical and emotional needs, a person feels better and is able to do more things by himself. For example, making healthy eating choices gives you energy to do many things to stay healthy and happy.

Eating nutritious foods can make you feel good physically and emotionally.

Do You Get It?

A need is something you must have to live. A want is something extra that you would like to have. Filling physical needs helps your body to stay healthy. Filling emotional needs helps you to stay healthy inside.

Knowing the difference between a want and need is also part of being healthy. Some things are both needs and wants. A warm coat is a need, but a warm coat that costs more than other coats is a want. People pay for many of their wants and needs with

When basic needs are met, people can feel healthy, safe, and happy.

THINK ABOUT IT

Make a list of the things you need each day and think about why they are needs. Then list your wants. Are there some things that are both needs and wants?

money they earn from jobs. Millions of people in the world do not have enough money to pay for their needs.

Needs and wants change because people and the world are changing. Age and ability are two things that affect your wants and needs. Your daily choices affect how you meet your needs and wants.

Many people who can meet their own needs try to help others do the same.

29

GLOSSARY

ability How people do things.

advertisement (ads) Something people see that helps to sell a good or service.

affect To cause something.

disabled Unable to do things like walking, seeing, hearing, or moving.

earn To get money from working.

emotional Having to do with how you feel.

expensive Costing a lot of money.

good Something that you can touch, like a book.

need Something a person must have to live.

physical Having to do with something you can see and touch.

respect Being treated well.

service Something that someone does for you, like cutting your hair.

shelter A place that gives protection, like a home.

supported Getting help, aid, or assistance.

technology The use of science to solve problems.

want Something a person would like to have but does not need.

wealthy Having a lot of money.

FOR MORE INFORMATION

Books

Berenstain, Jan, and Stan Berenstain. *The Berenstain Bears Get the Gimmies*. New York, NY: Random House Books for Young Readers, 1988.

Boelts, Maribeth. *Those Shoes*. Somerville, MA: Candlewick Press, 2009.

Bullard, Lisa. *Lily Learns About Wants and Needs*. Minneapolis, MN: Millbrook Press, 2013.

Larson, Jennifer. *Do I Need It? Or Do I Want It? Making Budget Choices*. Minneapolis, MN: Lerner Classroom, 2010.

Olson, Gillia. *Needs and Wants*. North Mankato, MN: Capstone Publishing, 2008.

Staniford, Linda. *Food and Drink (Wants versus Needs)*. Portsmouth, NH: Heinemann Publishing, 2015.

Websites

Because of the changing nature of Internet links, Rosen Publishing has developed an online list of websites related to the subject of this book. This site is updated regularly. Please use this link to access the list:

http://www.rosenlinks.com/LFO/wants

INDEX